G.

BE

DISC

ISBN 978-0-578-14101-5

GALVESTON: BEYOND THE BEACH

INSIDERS' GUIDE AND TIPS TO ISLAND FAVORITES

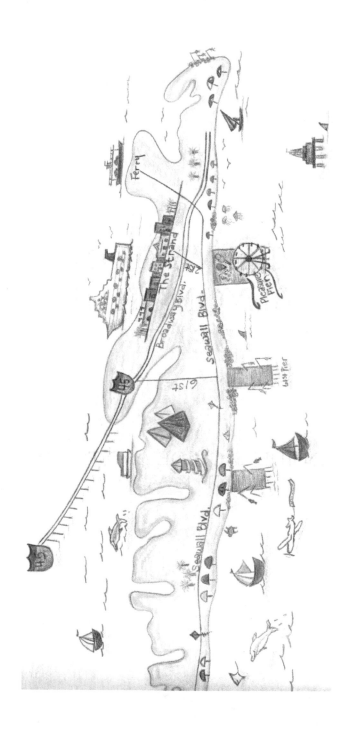

Contents

i

Introduction

While Galveston has been a major, national tourist destination for more than a hundred years, some of the Island's most overlooked features are among its most interesting! Remember that Galveston was once one of the leading ports in the U.S. and largest city in Texas, was home to a major Civil War battle (you can still see cannonball holes in some of the historic buildings) as well as wars between competing prohibition-era gangs, a wide open period of gambling and vice spanned into the mid-20th century spurred by the investments of a local crime family, and the Rat Pack called some of the more notorious fun spots along the sea their home away from home. With all that history, it always surprised us that Galveston has historically been viewed as "only" a beach destination. My mom and I love to travel, and we found over time that some of the best travel can be found close to home. We have lived in an around Galveston for more than 10 years, and have spent a lot of time poking into the various sunny, sandy, spooky, wet, dusty, delicious and beautiful spots the island has to offer. After all, while the

Galveston beaches are great for families, the real fun of Galveston can be found....beyond the beach! We have collected in this book what we think are some of the more interesting things you can do when you want to take a break from the beautiful views and warm seas, as well as additional resources you can use to identify great activities, terrific food and fun places to stay. Our hope is that you, like us, will fall in love with ALL that Galveston has to offer, and that no storm, economy or other forces have been able to sink.

———————

This book is dedicated to our wonderful husbands, Jeff and Jim, who believed we could accomplish our dreams and supported us every step of the way. And to Ethan and Delaney whose adventurous spirit, inspire those around them.

Annual Historic Homes Tour

During two weekends every May, you can catch a rare peek into Galveston's past. Different historic homes are showcased each year, and visitors can glimpse what it must have been like to live long ago in these stunning architectural treasures. Grab a map and take to the streets for a self guided tour of some of the most beautiful homes in Texas!

Local Tip: To see more, check the Galveston Historical Foundation's website for special events related to the Historic Homes Tour.

ARTOBERFEST

Every October, Galveston hosts Artoberfest, which features artists from near and far. Located in the historic downtown area, visitors can browse numerous tents in search of treasures. This weekend street festival features everything from jewelry and pottery, to photos and paintings, along with plenty of food and drink to keep you hunting for hours.

Local Tip: If you can't make Artoberfest, Galveston has art walks every six weeks or so throughout the year. While not as big as the festival, they will give you a wonderful introduction to the talented local artists who call the island home.

ASHTON VILLA

Finished in 1859, this grand home is considered to be the first of Broadway's "palaces," and is the first brick home built in Texas. Built by prominent businessman James M. Brown, a brick mason in his youth, it was separately commandeered for use during the Civil War by both the Confederate and the Union Armies. Mr. Brown had several children, his most famous child, Miss Bettie Brown, is said by some locals to still haunt the premises. Said to be a fiercely independent woman for her time and quite eccentric, Miss Bettie never married. Legend has it that she so loved being the "belle of the ball" that even to this day is unable to let go of the past.

Local Tip: This lovely home is not open for public tour but may be rented out for special occasions. You can also get a sneak peak of the grounds by visiting the Galveston Island Visitors Center which is located in the carriage house.

BISHOP'S PALACE

Just before you come to the end of Broadway Street, this mighty stone structure will surely catch your eye. The 1892 Bishop's Palace was built for the illustrious railroad magnate Walter Gresham, this ornate structure was so sturdily constructed that it weathered the famous 1900 hurricane with very little damage. Opulent and lavish, this Victorian masterpiece was purchased by the Galveston-Houston Catholic Archdiocese in 1923 and was home to Bishop Christopher Byrne - hence its moniker, Bishop's Palace. More recently this property was purchased by the Galveston Historical Foundation.

Local Tip: Bishop's Palace is open for tours, as well as photo shoots. Many local wedding photos are shot in this historic home.

Build a Sandcastle

Every spring teams of architects, designers, engineers and enthusiasts alike descend on East Beach to create some of the most amazing structures you will ever see, built entirely out of sand! The Houston Chapter of the American Institute of Architects has been hosting this event since 1986. While you may not win the highly coveted Golden Bucket award, you can grab your own shovel and plastic bucket and head to any of the area's local beaches to create your own masterpiece.

Local Tip: The AIA competition is incredibly popular. Locals avoid Saturday's large crowds and head over early on Sunday morning. You may miss some of the creative process, but the amazing sculptures won't disappoint.

COLLECT SEASHELLS

Galveston Island is considered one of the best beaches in the country for hunting seashells. Locals say that most favorable conditions are after a storm, when there is a northerly wind and at low tide, since those circumstances push the water off the sand and expose many varieties of beautiful seashells. While those may be the absolute ideal conditions, you can head to any local beach and enjoy finding shells anytime year 'round.

Local Tip: If you are interested in sharks' teeth, look for the area on the shore where the finest shells have washed up. Search closely around the tide line and you may find them - some as big as quarters!

DICKENS ON THE STRAND

Charles Dickens once said, "Happiness is a gift and the trick is not to expect it, but to delight in it when it comes." Delight the Victorian spirits of old do when Dickens on The Strand comes to Galveston. A nod to Dickens and an era long since past, this Victorian holiday festival takes place one glorious weekend every December in the Historic Strand. With parades, vendors, crafts, a petting zoo, snow, pub crawls, high tea, royalty, and five stages of entertainment to experience, this is the grand kickoff to the holiday season.

Local Tip: If it please thee, show up in Victorian era costume and receive half off the admission price. Thou wilst be in good company - many locals and visitors dress up for this grand weekend.

DIP YOUR TOE IN THE SURF

Beaches here are as different as the colorful birds that fill the Galveston Island skies. Many consider East Beach to be the "party" beach. Flocks of young people swarm to this beach because it is the only beach where alcohol is legal. In contrast, Stewart Beach is a more family-friendly environment. With a playground, water inflatables and snacks, the kids will play and be entertained for hours. Many smaller beaches dot the shores below the island's vast seawall, each with its own unique personality.

Local Tip: To get away from the crowds, head out to the west end of the island toward Galveston State Park. Many public beach access points dot the way, and the crowds will be a fraction of those at the larger beaches.

DRIVE A GO KART

Calling all racing fans! One of Galveston Island's newest attractions is of the four-wheeled variety. Just off Seawall Boulevard and 94th awaits the island's only go kart venue. Complete with an arcade, Galveston Go Karts offers a fun way to spend a few hours off the beach. The center provides picnic tables and birthday parties as well, so the next time you feel the need for speed, race to Galveston Go Karts.

Local Tip: The height requirement to ride is 56 inches for solo drivers, but double karts are available so smaller guests can enjoy the ride too!

EAT SHRIMP WITH THE LOCALS

Shrimp 'N Stuff has been a local favorite on the island since 1976. If you want to sit down and eat shrimp like the locals, this is the place to come. They boil them, fry them, stuff them, cover them with coconut, put them in soups and add them to salads. Make sure you show up early to nab a seat-yourself table here for lunch or dinner because this seafood spot fills up fast with locals, especially on weekends.

Local Tip: Sit on the patio and enjoy the soothing Gulf breezes!

EMPANADAS AND A GLASS OF WINE

A staple of many Latin American cultures, these tasty stuffed pastries are savory and delicious, especially when paired with a glass of red wine. Galveston Island is lucky to have some local folks who know how to make them right. Empanadas are made by folding dough around seafood, meat, cheese, or vegetables then baked or fried to create a perfect, steaming hot pastry package. Rudy & Paco (a popular local restaurant) offers "Empanadas Mixtas," which comes with a shrimp, beef and chicken empanada - in our opinion, the best on the island.

Local Tip: Rudy & Paco is located near The Grand Opera House and offers theatre dinning, so plan a night out! Grab some tickets to The Grand Opera House and enjoy a special meal before and be sure to make reservation in advance, because this fabulous restaurant fills up quickly, even during the week!

FEATHERFEST

If you are patient and ambitious enough, you have come to the right place to be a birder! Each April, bird lovers from all over the world gather on Galveston Island, a major migratory bird route. Here they celebrate their love of birds with workshops, outings, lectures, tours, and social events.

Local Tip: For the children in your life, Featherfest now offers Fledgling Fest, which exposes children to the world of birding through special lectures, bird walks, and interactive experiences.

FESTIVAL OF LIGHTS

If you head to Galveston between mid-November and early January, you will be dazzled by a spectacular display of over one million colorful Christmas lights adorning Moody Gardens. This winter wonderland comes complete with music, pictures with Santa, an outdoor ice skating rink, an artic slide, and hot cocoa. This vibrant experience is fun for kids and adults of every age.

Local Tip: On Fridays, Festival of Lights offers a "two for one" admission if you bring a non-perishable food item. All donations benefit the Galveston county and Houston food banks.

FIND A 1900 HURRICANE
SURVIVOR PLAQUE

On September 8 1900, under the cloak of darkness, one of the greatest natural disasters in U.S. history tore into Galveston with such force that it took at least 6,000 lives. Some reports state that as many as 12,000 souls perished in the wind and waves. As bridges washed away, so did the only hope of escaping the deadly Category 4 hurricane that descended upon them, with howling winds of up to 145 miles per hour. While much was lost on that fateful day, today surviving homes and businesses all over town wear plaques memorializing the storm, that gleam in the sunlight like a badges of honor.

Local Tip: For a list of all registered homes and businesses with plaques, head to the Galveston Historical Foundation.

FIND A ROSEATE
SPOONBILL

Although numerous in the early 1900s, this large, pink, and majestic coastal bird was hunted nearly to extinction by the 1930s, due to the demand for their coveted bright pink feathers for ladies' hats. Due to legal protection, these lovely birds are now making a comeback and can be seen feeding in our local marshy areas. Usually mistaken for flamingos (which do not live in Texas), these fascinating pink birds with long spoon-shaped bills are among the most unique birds that call Galveston Bay home.

Local Tip: To spot a Spoonbill, head to Galveston State Park on the bay side of the island, drive down Stewart Road and search the local ponds along either side, or try your luck behind the Target store (really!) on Broadway Street.

FIND A WHITE AND BROWN PELICAN

Galveston is considered one of the top birding spots in the country, and people travel from around the world to catch a glimpse of our year-round and migratory feathered friends. Although Galveston Island sits in the path of one of the major migration routes for birds, some of our favorites can be found here throughout the year. To find white and brown pelicans, merely look to the sky. You will find the white pelican with its striking black-tipped wings skimming local waters in search of fish, while the muddy colored brown pelican dives from great heights in search of dinner.

Local Tip: One of the best spots to see these birds up close is on the water behind Joe's Crab Shack on Pier 19.

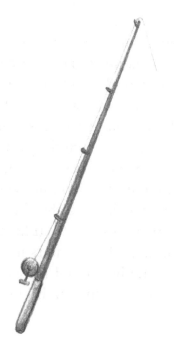

FISH OFF A PIER

Hundreds of years ago, abundant sea and fish life attracted the Karankawa Indians to the local waters surrounding Galveston Island. Today, people still flock to the murky waters of the gulf in hopes of catching a sand trout, stingray, redfish or even an elusive shark. Local piers offer rental rods, tackle and bait, along with snacks and refreshments to aid you in your search for the great white whale.

Local Tip: The 61st street pier and Galveston fishing pier are two local favorite spots. Both offer rentals and supplies. Jimmy's on the Pier, located on the Galveston fishing pier, has an espresso bar and serves delicious food all day.

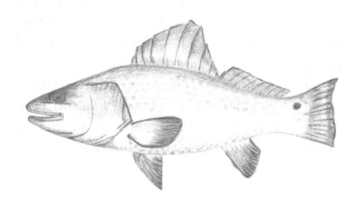

FISH THE GULF WATERS

Fishing enthusiasts will feel right at home in the fish filled waters surrounding Galveston. Venture offshore into the bluish green waves in search of sharks, kingfish, red snapper, tuna, wahoo, sailfish, and much more! Whether you opt for a quick trip to Mitchell's reef or an all day adventure into the great blue yonder, Galveston offers many charters for every budget and need.

Local Tip: For an afordable option check out Capt. Johns boat. Third generation fisherman, they know where to find the fish. Also provided is all tackle and bait.

FLY A KITE

Galveston is a breezy kite lover's paradise. With plenty of open spaces to take advantage of the wind, you can indulge your dreams of flying nearly anywhere on the island. Check out Kites Unlimited, located at 89th and Seawall, where you will enter a store more colorful than a coral reef. Surrounded by kites of all shapes and sizes, pick your favorite and head to the beach for an afternoon of fun.

Local Tip: Continue down Seawall towards Pirate's Beach (on the west end) to Hummel's General Store & Deli, where you can grab a delicious picnic lunch to accompany your day of kite flying.

GALVESTON ART WALK

For more than 20 years, locals and artists have been coming together in the name of art. Every six weeks or so on Saturday nights, the local galleries of the historic downtown area of Galveston are open to shoppers. Most artists are happy to interact and answer questions you may have about their work. Whether you're looking for something small or for a grand masterpiece, you will find an abundance of treasures around every corner.

Local Tip: Many art galleries offer free wine and snacks during this event.

GALVESTON CUSTOM HOUSE (1861)

In 1861, construction of the Galveston Custom House was finished on the eve of what would become the deadliest war to be fought on U.S. soil, the Civil War. Throughout the years, this mighty brick Greek-Revival building has functioned as a customs house for one of the nation's busiest ports, a post office, a courthouse and even the site of the 1864 "bread riot" initiated by wives of absent confederate soldiers demanding flour for their bread. It is now home to the Galveston Historical Foundation, which has been instrumental in the on-going preservation of Galveston Island and its captivating history.

Local Tip: If you are looking to enhance your island experience with historical information then check out Galveston Historical Foundation's website to learn about upcoming events and special tours.

GALVESTON FOOD AND WINE FESTIVAL

With delicious samples from local restaurants and wines from around the world, this ever-expanding and popular event is an island favorite. Held every April in historic downtown Galveston, this festival features premium wine and food pairings, blind tastings, the grand tasting (with live music), souvenir wine glasses, and endless food and wine samples.

Local Tip: Please drink responsibly. There are many wonderful hotels within walking distance of this event, including the historic Tremont House Hotel and The Harbor House at Pier 21, so there is no need to drive.

GALVESTON HURRICANE MEMORIAL

Along the Seawall, sits a bronzed family, reaching toward the sky, forever frozen in time. Installed in 2000 to mark the 100 year anniversary of The Great Storm, this stunning statue by Galveston artist David W. Moore, honors the victims and survivors alike of the devastating September 8, 1900 Galveston hurricane. Pause for a moment of silence, while gazing into the vast ocean, in remembrance of all the men, woman and children who lost their lives on that fateful day in September.

Local Tip: A great book to read while lounging on the beach is, *Isaac's Storm: A Man, a Time, and the Deadliest Hurricane in History* by Erik Larson.

GALVESTON ISLAND BREWING

Thanks to recent changes in Texas law, our very own craft brewery and pub is now open on Galveston Island. Come and enjoy local brews at the beautiful copper bar, or bring a growler and take some delicious craft beer to your next party. Owner Mark Dell 'Osso offers weekend tours as well.

Local Tip: Located outside is a sitting area which faces the setting sun, so grab a pint and relax while the day slips into night.

GALVESTON ISLAND
HISTORIC PLEASURE PIER

Originally built in the early 1940s, the pleasure pier was destroyed by Hurricane Carla in 1961. In its place, the Flagship Hotel was constructed and stood until Hurricane Ike blew into town and damaged it beyond repair. From the "ashes" rose the Pleasure Pier (which extends 1,130 feet into the gulf waters). This one-of-a-kind Texas amusement park offers rides, midway games, live music, and food, all with an unforgettable waterfront view.

Local Tip: Be warned that the Pleasure Pier is pricey, and you must pay just to walk on even if you don't ride. The best value is to buy an all-day pass (which allows you to come and go from the pier) and plan on using it from open to close.

GALVESTON ISLAND
HISTORIC TOURS

A twelve-person electric shuttle leaves daily from the Galveston Island Visitor's Center, located at 2328 Broadway behind Aston Villa. In good weather, touring in this open air vehicle is a great way to see the island and learn some history narrated by one of Galveston Islands' locals. Sit back and relax as you spend an hour or so discovering downtown, Broadway, the Historic Strand, and many other interesting historical sites.

Local Tip: The Galveston Island Visitor's Center is a great place to begin your adventure. They offer invaluable information about local events, as well as brochures on area attractions.

GALVESTON RAILROAD
MUSEUM

All aboard! Step back in time at this fascinating museum that pays homage to Galveston's railroad past. Your adventure begins when you pass through the "portal" and enter a grand room filled with statues of people depicting a bygone era. Full of interesting exhibits, hands-on activities, and trains you can actually board, this family-friendly museum awaits you at the end of the Historic Strand.

Local Tip: In December kids of all ages can enjoy the Santa Train and Polar Express.

GALVESTON STATE PARK

Located roughly 13 miles down Galveston Island is its state park, a lovely oasis. Part of the Texas Parks and Wildlife Department, it offers campsites, hiking trails, kayaking, bird watching, wildlife viewing, fishing, beach activities, and guided tours and programs. In the spring months into early summer, nesting sea turtles come to shore so keep a close eye out for these amazing creatures and immediately alert the Park Ranger of any sightings.

Local Tip: Galveston State Park offers the "tackle loaner program" which allows you to borrow fishing gear to use within the state park.

GARTEN VEREIN (1880)

As if plucked from a magical German forest, this unique octagonal building lies nestled like a beautiful rare gem amid Kempner Park. Built in 1880 for the German community in Galveston, this social "garden club" was an oasis for those homesick for the motherland. It served the finest German beer and food to be had. Bought by Stanley Kempner in 1923 and donated to the city of Galveston, one can still imagine the traditional drinking song, *Ein Prosit* spilling from the octagonal hall's open windows.

Local Tip: Although Garten Verein is available only for private functions and is not open to the public for tours, enter Kempner Park during daylight hours to get a closer look.

GHOST TOUR

Whether or not you believe in ghosts, local lore tells of spirits that drift amidst the dark Galveston sea breezes. Throughout history, many have perished on the island and legends have grown like the waves of an approaching hurricane. Whether touring the Historic Strand with its turn of the century buildings, roaming the dark misty Seawall, or creeping through the old city cemetery, - stop - listen, and close your eyes. Perhaps ghosts of yesteryear are near at hand.

Local Tip: Nationally known local Dash Beardsley offers ghost tours of Galveston year 'round. During the month of October, the Galveston Historic Foundation offers special "haunting" tours as well.

GRAB A CUP OF GUMBO

This delicious cup of goodness originated in Louisiana during the 18th century. Always containing the Cajun "trinity" of celery, onion and bell pepper, gumbos are as different as the people who create them. Some use okra while others prefer file. Some like seafood, and others only fowl or sausage. Some serve it over rice and others like it plain. However you like your gumbo, be sure to grab a cup while in Galveston, and see what the locals have been enjoying for years.

Local Tip: Gumbo can be found at almost every seafood restaurant on the island. While there are many tasty concoctions, our favorite is at the Gumbo Bar.

HAUNTED MAYFIELD
MANOR

Ghosts of Galveston's past are reaching out from beyond the grave along the Historic Strand. Haunted Mayfield Manor beckons those who dare to step foot over its threshold. Dr. Mayfield welcomes all into his manor, where the horrors of 12 terrifying rooms await. This is not for the faint of heart - enter at your own risk!

Local Tip: This year 'round haunted house is all in good fun but might be too scary for kids under the age of 12.

HENDLEY BUILDING

Finished in 1860, the historic Hendley building is the oldest remaining commercial building on The Strand. Originally built for brothers Joseph and William Hendley to serve as office space, later it became a Confederate watchtower during the Civil War. Cannonball damage can still be seen from the 1863 Battle of Galveston on the 20th Street side of the building.

Local Tip: Many historic buildings are located in the Historic Strand District. To take a self-guided walking tour simply start at one end of the strand and you will find historic markers along the way full of fascinating information.

HOTEL GALVEZ

The palm-lined entrance of the stunning historic Hotel Galvez dates back to 1911, when her doors first opened. This magnificent hotel has been host to Presidents and celebrities alike, but there is one guest you may not wish to encounter. Legend has it the Ghost Bride of Room 501 hung herself when she feared her sailor fiancé was lost at sea. It is said that her restless soul still roams the halls, calling his name.

Local Tip: Check out the basement of the Hotel Galvez. Here you will find pictures and artifacts from Galveston's past, when it was known by those near and far as "The Queen City of the Gulf."

HUNT FOR NAUTICAL "TREASURE"

Venture off the main street of the Historic Strand to hunt for nautical treasure and you will find some true gems. Our favorite, Nautical Antiques, is located at 2202 Ship Mechanic Row. There you will find salvaged items from shipyards all over the world - from ships wheels to flags, glass balls, life rings, oars, plates, pictures and so much more. You can spend hours seeking salvaged treasure in this wondrous warehouse.

Local Tip: Check the seasonal hours before you head out shopping, since they are closed mid-week and their hours vary between summer and winter months.

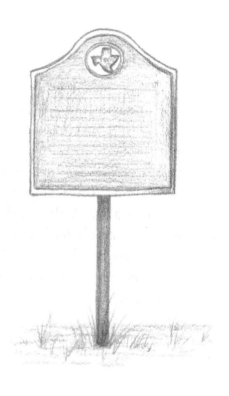

KARANKAWA INDIAN CAMPSITE AND BURIAL GROUND

The great Karankawa tribe once called the Gulf Coast home. Tall and tattooed, this mysterious tribe allegedly practiced ceremonial cannibalism. Buried deep within the earth of the island, many artifacts surely remain. If you head down Galveston Island to the community of Jamaica Beach, you will encounter a historical marker that pays tribute to their one-time campsite and burial ground that was discovered in 1962.

Local Tip: Stop in for a bite to eat at Blue Water Grill. It is a local favorite in Jamaica Beach and serves up delicious pizza and burgers.

KATIE'S SEAFOOD MARKET

In a tin shack supported by pilings over the water, can be found the best seafood market in Galveston. Head to Pier 19 then take a hard right towards a small marina on Wharf Road, and you will find this hidden gem. The majority of their seafood comes from local fisherman and shrimpers, fresh from the Gulf waters surrounding Galveston Island. Katie's Market supplies many area restaurants but is open to the public too. You will find the very freshest gulf snapper, blue crab, flounder, shrimp and grouper, just to name a few.

Local Tip: Headed back home? They will clean and filet your fish and pack it on ice.

THE KITCHEN CHICK

Located in downtown Galveston, The Kitchen Chick is a fun and quirky store. Loaded with gourmet kitchen wares, sea themed items, local books and art, this one stop kitchen shop is a must visit on your island getaway. The Kitchen Chicks inventory changes with the seasons, providing the opportunity to purchase fun gifts for friends and family.

Local Tip: A variety of cooking classes are offered at The Kitchen Chick throughout the year. Check her wesbiste to see what is currently available.

LONE STAR RALLY

Every year, bikers from all over the country rumble south for warm weather and camaraderie. Brought together by their love of motorcycles and the mild Texas fall, hundreds of thousands gather for a weekend of fun, contests, poker runs, exhibitions, and bikini contests. Next year when winter is knocking on your door, remember the Lone Star Rally and the biker saying that four wheels move the body, but two wheels move the soul.

Local Tip: Nearly 500,000 people attend this event, so book well in advance or you'll have no chance at finding a place to lay your head. Many from the surrounding counties rent beach houses in nearby Pirates Beach or Jamaica Beach in lieu of hotel rooms. Contact Sand 'N Sea Rentals for listings of rental properties.

LOOK FOR BURIED
TREASURE

Legend has it that beneath the ever shifting sand dunes of hurricane ravaged Galveston Island awaits the treasure of the notorious pirate Jean Lafitte. While time and weather are against you, it is thought that the pirate's treasure sleeps deep in the earth, waiting to see the light of day once again. Jean Lafitte called Galveston Island home from 1815 to 1821, and it is said that he hid his spoils in many locations around Galveston. So next time you dig that sandcastle or plant a tree, dig just a little further and see what waits for thee.

Local Tip: Academy Sports + Outdoors, located between Fort Crockett Boulevard and the Seawall, offers many beach items needed for a fun filled day – including shovels to help dig for buried treasure!

MAGIC CARPET MINI GOLF

Located on Seawall Boulevard, this magical mini golf haven has been providing family fun for years. Locals and tourist alike will enjoy the whimsical and fun holes, such as the giant turtle and the conch shell. Gulf breezes help keep you cool through all 18 holes of entertainment and the view over the water, particularly around sun set, is peaceful and serene.

Local Tip: They don't accept credit cards, so be sure to bring cash.

MARDI GRAS

The Galveston Mardi Gras story dates back to 1867, when a masked ball and a production of Shakespeare's "King Henry IV" came to town. While Galveston marched on, the parties and celebrations waxed and waned through the decades. George P. Mitchell and his wife Cynthia revived the citywide party in 1985. Not only is Galveston's Mardi Gras the largest in Texas, but many of the Island's communities feature unique opportunities to revel, with elaborate floats, thousands of colorful beads, kid-friendly events, live music, and fun.

Local Tip: Want to join a parade? Decorate an umbrella and groove along the downtown entertainment area with the Funky Umbrella Brigade.

Moody Gardens

Moody Gardens is an enormous complex right in the heart of Galveston. This hotel and golf course development is a family destination featuring three giant glass pyramids that rise into the sky to welcome visitors. The first holds an aquarium, an aquatic home to sharks, penguins and fish from all over the world. The second pyramid showcases an imposing Rainforest, with beautiful birds and animals from near and far. The third pyramid houses a discovery museum, which offers traveling exhibits for people of all ages to explore and enjoy. With its hotel, golf course, zip line and ropes course, 3D theater, 4D theater, a ride film, Colonel Paddlewheel Boat that cruises on beautiful Offats Bayou, Moody Gardens epitomizes family fun!

Local Tip: Moody Gardens offers behind the scenes penguin encounters. Go online to reserve your spot before visiting.

MOODY MANSION

Like a grand dame beckoning visitors from her throne, the Moody Mansion regally sits at 26th and Broadway. Completed in 1895, the property was acquired by the Moody family in 1900, shortly after The Great Storm. Legend has it that the ever-gifted businessman William Lewis Moody got the elegant mansion for a "steal" since many were fleeing the island in the wake of Mother Nature's destruction. The Moody family spent decades enjoying the impressive 28,000 square foot home, which was opened for public tours in 1991.

Local Tip: Moody Mansion is available for daily tours, as well as private rentals and special events.

MURDOCH'S
"BATHHOUSE"

The original bathhouse was first built in Galveston in the late 1800s. For mere pennies, visitors could rent bathing suits and showers for a quick rinse after a day in the hot Texas sun. Mother Nature had different plans, however, and in 1900 The Great Storm swept into Galveston and took the original bath house out to sea. Murdoch's was rebuilt and destroyed numerous times over the next hundred years, with Hurricane Ike being the most recent storm to swallow it up. Rebuilt once again after that 2008 storm but no longer a bathhouse, Murdoch's sits over the sand, paying homage to its past, inviting Galveston visitors inside to buy its island wares.

Local Tip: Murdoch's now serves beer and frozen drinks, so sit back and relax on the back deck while gazing out into the Gulf.

OCEAN STAR OFFSHORE DRILLING RIG & MUSEUM

Whether you agree or disagree with drilling Gulf oil, this retired jack-up drilling rig is now a unique museum offering a fascinating inside look at the drilling industry and its history. With hands-on exhibits and interactive displays, information about geological exploration, and insights on oil and gas production, you will come away educated about these giant steel beasts that call our backyard home.

Local Tip: When crossing the skywalk onto the rig check out the brown and white pelicans who like to sit on the rocks and watch the people walk by. This is one of the best places on Galveston to get an up close view of the magnificent birds.

OHANA SURF AND SKATE

You don't have to hop a plane to Cali or Hawaii to learn to surf or skateboard. Galveston Island's finest surf and skate shop offers lessons in surfing, skating, and paddle boarding. During summer months, learn to surf in the shadow of the Pleasure Pier or book a catered birthday party (for youths and adults) and enjoy a fun and active day in the warm Galveston sun.

Local Tip: Ohana Surf and Skate has a cool selection of beach clothing, shoes, and gear, so stop in and shop next time you are passing by on Seawall Boulevard.

OLD CITY CEMETERY

As you make your way towards the sea along Broadway Street, listen closely for a low moaning voice as you approach the old city cemetery. Some say it is the howling of the wind, while others claim it is the screams of Thomas "Nicaragua" Smith, a civil war soldier who was executed and buried in an unmarked grave deep in the heart of the cemetery. Either way, this historic resting place can be an eerily beautiful site, especially in the spring, when blooming yellow wildflowers cover the ground.

Local Tip: Several area businesses offer ghost tours in the cemetery. Call them – if you dare!

"OLD RED" AT UTMB MEDICAL CENTER

The Ashbel Smith Building, known as "Old Red," sits on the campus of the University of Texas Medical Branch in Galveston like a beautiful pearl encompassed by a less than dazzling shell. Built in 1891, this gorgeous Romanesque Revival structure gets its name from the red brick and sandstone used in its construction. When first opened, this building housed the entire medical school under its impressive roof. Although concrete structures now proliferate around this historic building, "Old Red" stands as a reminder of this campus' historic beginnings and is the oldest surviving medical school building west of the Mississippi River.

Local Tip: Grab a bite to eat at one of the many great restaurants located around the UTMB campus. With its fun and relaxing patio, Smooth Tony's is our favorite.

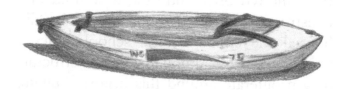

PADDLE A KAYAK

Head to Galveston State Park and - like the Karankawa Indians did in centuries past - launch a kayak into the gentle waters of the inland coastal waterways. Kayak paddling tours are conducted every Saturday on the bay side of the Galveston State Park, from April to November at 10 a.m. They are on a first-come-first served basis, but you can also arrange for tours on other days by contacting the state park directly.

Local Tip: To venture further into the numerous surrounding waterways, contact local company artist boat for private tours.

PIER 21 THEATER

Here in the dark, three historic tales unfold before your eyes. First, is the tale of the catastrophic 1900 *Great Storm* that forever changed Galveston. The second, *The Pirate Island of Jean Laffite,* questions whether this infamous man in the black hat was, a hero or a villain. The last, *Gateway to the Gulf,* examines one hundred years of immigration through Galveston, 1835-1935, where more than 200,000 people first stepped foot on U.S. soil. All shows are priced separately and start either on the hour or on the half hour.

Local Tip: The newest show, *Gateway to the Gulf,* currently runs at 10 a.m. and 4 p.m. (due to its near-hour running time), so plan accordingly if you are interested in seeing this one along with the others.

PIRATES! LEGENDS OF THE GULF COAST

Many adventurers have called Galveston home over the centuries, but none is more infamous than the pirate Jean Lafitte. Young and old alike will enjoy a peek into this small museum to learn about the history of pirates along the Gulf Coast. With interactive hands on exhibits for children and memorabilia to explore, this is a great place to spend an hour surrounded by pirate lore.

Local Tip: Pirates! Legends of the Gulf Coast offers pirate camps as well as children's birthday parties. Call to reserve your spot!

RAISE A PINT AT OKTOBERFEST

Every year on the fourth Saturday in October, Galveston's First Lutheran Church pays homage to its German roots with an Oktoberfest celebration for 15,000 of its closest friends. Founded by German immigrants in 1850, the local church started its Oktoberfest festivities in 1981. Today it has grown into an island favorite that boasts live German music, authentic food and strudels, and both local beers and German style brews such as Paulaner and Hofbrau. Admission is free, and many locals dress in traditional German attire.

Local Tip: Be sure to visit the historic church lyceum, with its gorgeous stained glass windows and vaulted wood beam ceiling. This area is set up with booths selling local wares and crafts from around the world.

RIDE A FERRY FOR FREE!

Where else can you see scores of sea birds dancing on the wind and dolphins playing in the wake among ocean-going vessels that hail from far across the sea? The Galveston-Port Bolivar Ferry began carrying people from Galveston Island to the Bolivar Peninsula in 1929. This 2.7 mile trip takes a mere 18 minutes each way and is completely free of charge. Unique to the Texas coast, this scenic and romantic crossing is operated by the Texas Department of Transportation.

Local Tip: The ferries are busiest in the months of June, July and August, when waiting times can reach into the hours. Instead of waiting in the car line, park in the visitors' lot and walk onto the ferry. When you reach the other side, simply stay on the ferry and ride it back.

ROSENBERG LIBRARY
(1871)

The bronzed statue of a local business man and book lover Henry Rosenberg, sits proudly keeping watch over his namesake, as if welcoming people of all ages into one of the oldest public libraries in Texas. With a wide selection of adult books and an enchanting children's area (complete with computers, animals and a treasure hunt) this site offer virtually everyone a place to relax. But... like many historic buildings, this library has a rare gem hidden away. On the top floor, a local museum awaits those interested in the history of Galveston. Giant ships wheels, paintings, and artifacts from bygone eras bring local legends and facts to life.

Local Tip: Slightly used books are available for purchase on the second floor for a steal!

RUINS OF PIRATE JEAN LAFITTE'S HOME

"Yo ho, yo ho, a pirate's life for me!" Those words linger on the thick morning air sweeping in from shore over the ruins of the pirate Jean Lafitte's fortress, Maison Rouge (Red House), located on Harborside Drive between 14th and 15th Street (look for the stone ruins and historic marker). The privateer-turned pirate Jean Lafitte called Galveston home from 1815-1821 until the United States government demanded the mighty pirate leave the island. He sailed away, but he burned this fortress to the ground in a final act of defiance.

Local Tip: There is no parking or stopping on Harborside Drive so turn onto 14th Street and park. You will find a historic marker with information about Jean Lafitte located in the corner of the lot.

SACRED HEART CHURCH

Anyone who has ever driven down Broadway to the Gulf of Mexico can never forget the sight of this massive white beacon of hope shining in the sun and surrounded by towering palm trees. First built in 1884, this French Romanesque Church was destroyed by The Great Storm of 1900; all that remained of it were two stained glass windows, the mass bell, a crucifix and the Sacred Heart statue. Its rebuilding began in 1904, and the brilliantly white church sits today in all its glory, for everyone to enjoy.

Local Tip: The church is open for mass on Sundays if you are interested in attending.

SCHLITTERBAHN WATER PARK

Summer is an ideal time to visit this awesome water park, but if your travels take you to Galveston in the winter then bring your swim suit and revel in this water park's heated indoor season! Summer adventures include daring to ride the Cliffhanger, Dragon Blaster, or the Twin Twister. When winter blankets Texas, move indoors to the heated enclosed water adventures and enjoy summer fun even during the cold winter months. Visit in December, and you'll see that even Santa himself can't resist a ride on the Boogie Bahn surf ride!

Local Tip: Cabanas are offered during summer months and are well worth the extra price. Reserve them online at Schlitterbahn.com.

SEARCH THROUGH
SEAWEED

Every year, thousands of visitors descend on Galveston beaches in the spring and summer months - only to find globs of brown seaweed covering the beaches. Unfortunately, there is nothing that can be done about these large naturally-occurring masses, but the silver lining is that they are home to many types of sea life. Grab a beach pail, fill it with water, gently drop in a bunch of seaweed, stir, then look closely. You will find fish, crabs, shrimp, and even baby seahorses and turtles hidden among the watery branches. When life gives you seaweed, make a mobile aquarium! When you are done investigating these wonders of marine life, please remember to return the animals to their Gulf home.

Local Tip: If you happen to find a sea turtle call NOAA at 1-866-887-8535 for information on how best to handle it.

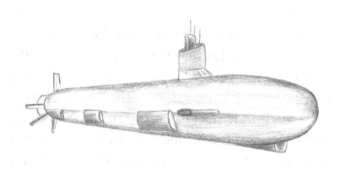

SEAWOLF PARK

If you want something truly unique for your next family outing, then head over to Seawolf Park for a day of fun. You will find a lighted fishing pier, a plethora of picnic areas, a large playground, and - oh yeah - a submarine and a destroyer escort! Climb aboard the USS Stewart (one of only three destroyer escorts in the world) then submerge in the USS Cavalla, (a Gato class fleet submarine), be forewarned - it is a tight squeeze if you are claustrophobic. Seawolf Park gives you an opportunity to relax and enjoy a unique piece of naval history found only in Galveston.

Local Tip: There is no food on site, so don't forget to bring something to munch on as you get a glimpse into our nation's history.

SEGCITY SEGWAY TOURS

Picture yourself on a Segway, touring Galveston Island as though you're starring in a movie scene from some futuristic thriller. A Segway tour is a fun and safe way to move around the island! Learn about historic mansions that withstood the wrath of the Great Storm of 1900, see fabulous works of art made from oak trees felled by Hurricane Ike, and find out why the famous Rat Pack flew halfway across the country to party here. Rest a few minutes and watch a beautiful sunset, or hear tales of ghosts floating through the dark and stormy skies.

Local Tip: SegCity Segway Tours is open for business seven days a week, but tours are by appointment only. Departure times vary by weekdays and weekends and also depend on which tour you choose. After a quick lesson, you will be on your way to explore, ride, and learn on this unique, and unforgettable adventure!

SHOP THE HISTORIC STRAND DISTRICT

Designated as a National Historic Landmark in 1976, the Historic Strand District is Galveston's premier market-style shopping haven. Here you will find quaint stores, restaurants, bars, art galleries and museums, many of which are housed in Victorian era buildings dating as far back as 1855. In many shops and restaurants, you will find plaques marking the 2008 water line from Hurricane Ike.

Local Tip: Head to Saengerfest Park (located in the middle of the Historic Strand), where you will find park benches and a giant playable chess set, for relaxation and play.

SILK STOCKING DISTRICT

Believed to have derived its name from its reputation as home to the prosperous families of old Galveston, this historic district has some excellent examples of Queen Anne style architecture. The Silk Stocking district sits between Seawall Boulevard and Broadway; its boundaries being 25th Street (west), 23rd Street (east), Avenue P (south) and Avenue K (north).

Local Tip: Log onto the Silk Stocking Galveston website and print out a walking/driving tour of the neighborhood. It provides the location and history of many of the fine homes in this district.

SPOT A DOLPHIN

Although hundreds of bottlenose dolphins live in the waters surrounding Galveston, you need to know where to look to get a peek at these playful sea mammals. Our local dolphins love to follow the shrimp boats, swim in the bay, and play in the wakes created by the giant ocean-going ships visiting the Port of Houston. If you don't have a boat, your best bet of seeing one of these amazing creatures is to hop on the Bolivar ferry, from which they can usually be seen riding the bow wake. Another great place to catch a glimpse is from the pavilion in Sea Wolf Park, located at the end of 51st Street on Pelican Island.

Local Tip: Baywatch Dolphin Tours is a family-owned company that provides affordable 45-minute tours that leave from Pier 21. Dolphins are wild animals and go where they choose, but if they are out there, Baywatch Dolphin Tours will find them for you!

St. Joseph's Church

Built in 1860, this quaint church is the oldest German Catholic Church in Texas and the oldest wooden church in Galveston. In the mid-1800s, Galveston was a major port of entry for German immigrants. Many moved inland to places like New Braunfels, but those who stayed helped build St. Joseph's Church. Although severely damaged in The Great Storm of 1900, the church was quickly restored to its former glory. Closed by the Diocese of Galveston-Houston in 1968, its contents were sold at public auction. Hearing that it was to be used as a warehouse, the Galveston Historical Foundation stepped in, leased the property and recovered most of the contents. The GHF continues to maintain this building, which is sometimes opened for group tours.

Local Tip: This church can be rented for private functions through the Galveston Historical Foundation.

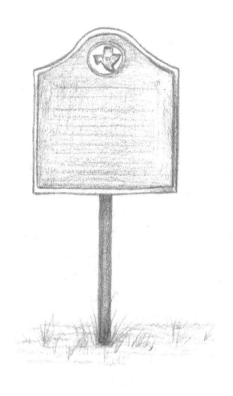

St. Mary's Orphan Asylum Historical Marker

At 69th Street and Seawall Boulevard marks the spot of the old orphanage that was once home to the 10 nuns and 90 children who perished during The Great Storm on September 8, 1900. As the brave nuns sang the old French hymn, "Queen of the Waves," they tied themselves to the children with clothesline in an attempt to save their young lives. As they sang, the waves crashed over them and carried their souls away. Only three boys, who were swept out to sea, survived. To this day, no matter where they are in the world, the Sisters of Charity of the Incarnate Word look to the heavens each September 8 and sing to honor their sisters and the children whose lives were taken by the unrelenting and ferocious waves.

Local Tip: To learn more about Galveston Island's history and lore head to the Historic Strand where many shop owners carry books on the subject.

STAR DRUG STORE (1886)

Step back in time at this fun and funky old-fashioned restaurant and soda fountain. From mouthwatering breakfasts like grandma used to make to sandwiches and burgers hot off the grill, here's a great place to pop into while visiting Galveston Island. Sit at the restaurant's centerpiece, a giant olde tyme soda fountain where you can sip on a shipwreck float or enjoy a banana split and harken back to simpler times.

Local Tip: When you are finished eating, be sure to head upstairs to the catwalk, where you can discover fun artwork at very reasonable prices.

TAKE A DUCK TOUR

Calling kids of all ages - time to board the quackmobile! While you may question whether this silly looking amphibious ride is worth a spin, we are here to tell you to let loose and hop on! Your knowledgeable driver will tell you the history of Galveston Island while you are cruising the Seawall, seeing historic homes, waddling down the Historic Strand, and plunging into the waters of Offatts Bayou. Located at 25th and Seawall Boulevard, this fun excursion is open year 'round.

Local Tip: If you are part of a large party (up to 24 people) save some money and rent the whole duck!

TAKE A STROLL ON THE SEAWALL

Following the devastating storm of 1900, the city put a plan into motion to save the town from future storms. Not only did the massive Seawall begin its protection of the city, but it created a grand "boardwalk" still enjoyed today. Stretching for miles, this concrete promenade is home to stores, restaurants, hotels and even rollercoasters.

Local Tip: You will find the world's longest mural located between 27th and 61st Streets, running along the front face of the seawall. Designed by local artist Peter Davis, the colorful murals depicts marine life, birds, and local Galveston attractions.

TASTY TEX-MEX

Combine the words Texan and Mexican, and you'll come up with the name for one of the most popular styles of food anywhere! You will find many restaurants in Galveston serving this popular local cuisine, but the trick is finding the very best ones. From sizzling fajitas to cheesy nachos and enchiladas, queso and quesadillas, and of course the ever-refreshing margarita (with or without salt), there is something for everyone when you head out to eat Tex-Mex!

Local Tip: A local island favorite is The Original Mexican Café, which has been serving up tasty Tex-Mex dishes since 1916.

TEE OFF

Jack Benny once said, "Give me the fresh air, a beautiful partner, and a nice round of golf, and you can keep the fresh air and the round of golf." No offense, Jack, but when you come to the first-rate Moody Gardens golf course, you can have them *all*. Set among swaying palm trees, native tropical plants and exotic local birds (like the Roseate Spoonbill), this public golf course is the perfect spot to tee off on your Island adventure.

Local Tip: If you rent a house in Pirates Beach, many of the rental agreements come with privileges at the Galveston Country Club, which boasts an attractive private golf course.

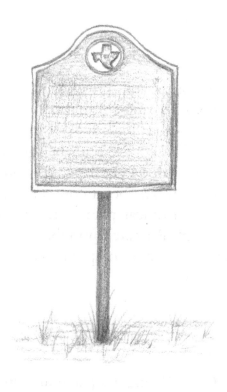

TEXAS HEROES
MONUMENT

High upon granite columns, at Broadway and 25th, a bronze figure of Winged Victory proudly points across the bay towards the San Jacinto Battleground. Given to the City of Galveston and the people of Texas by business leader and philanthropist Henry Rosenberg, this statue pays tribute to the heroes of the Texas Revolution. Made by Italian sculptor Louis Amateis and dedicated on April 21, 1900, she will forever stand as a monument and reminder of those heroes who came before us.

Local Tip: If you are interested in learning more about the San Jacinto Battleground, it is located approximately 45 minutes north of Galveston and is open to visitors 7 days a week. It is home to a museum, library, monument, Battleship Texas and the Battleground.

TEXAS SEAPORT MUSEUM

Home of the 1877 tall ship *Elissa*, the Texas Seaport Museum is much more than just a lovely three-masted iron-hulled ship – it's a floating National Historic Landmark! Its museum and theater tell the fascinating story of the *Elissa's* rescue from a scrapyard in Greece and its tedious restoration. The museum also recounts the history of immigration in Galveston. Known as "The Ellis Island of the West," more than 200,000 immigrants set their first foot on American soil right here on Galveston Island.

Local Tip: Many special events and "behind the scenes" tours are available at the Texas Seaport Museum. Check out their website to see what is available while you are visiting.

The Grand 1894 Opera House

Truly one of Galveston Island's finest gems, this historic opera house survived the Great Storm of 1900 and is listed on the National Register of Historic Places. This cultural cornerstone showcases every form of entertainment, including opera, ballet, theater, children's programs and workshops, Christmas shows, country music, the blues, and much more.

Local Tip: If you don't have time to take in a show, take the self-guided tour (offered daily) and discover why the Texas legislature proclaimed this site, "the official Opera House of Texas."

TREASURE ISLE TOUR TRAIN

Step aboard this bright pink open air trolley and step back in time to learn more about the fascinating history of Galveston Island. This 90-minute tour will give you a new appreciation for the local lore of this multi-faceted island. Sit back, and relax as you tour homes and sites from bygone eras, learn how the devastating storm of 1900 forever changed the island, and how Hurricane Ike created great works of art.

Local Tip: Stop in at Fish Tales before or after your tour, it is located just across the street, and try the famous Texas Blue Bell Ice Cream.

TREE SCULPTURE TOUR

On September 13, 2008, Hurricane Ike swept into town and flooded the island with its massive storm surge, uprooting and killing more than 35,000 of the island's beautiful trees. In the aftermath of this devastation, residents came together and paid for the lifeless trees to be transformed into stunning works of art. Explore these works that have gone from trees to treasures – now in the form of dolphins, owls, mermaids, birds, and more.

Local Tip: A self-guided map tour of all the tree sculpture art is available at the Galveston Island Information Center, located at Aston Villa. Galveston Island Tours offer Saturday guided tours in their solar powered bus, too!

TREMONT HOUSE HOTEL

Sitting in quiet elegance at one end of the Historic Strand, this grand hotel oozes sophistication and charm. Located in the 1879 Leon and H. Blum Building, the Tremont House Hotel beckons weary travelers into its charming lobby to relax at the restored Toujouse Bar that dates back to 1888. With its warm and cheery rooms, there is no better place on the island to lay your head after exploring all that Galveston has to offer.

Local Tip: The rooftop bar at the Tremont is a great place to grab a drink and enjoy the views, especially during sunset.

TRY SOME LOCAL TAFFY

Right in the heart of the Historic Strand is a candy store and ice cream shop that will transport you back in time. La King's Confectionery offers everything a sweet tooth could desire – and more. Using 19th century formulas and methods handed down from his father James H. King, Jack King carries on the family tradition with delicious results, offering candies of all shapes, colors, sizes and flavors. Its 1920 soda fountain features Purity ice cream (founded in Galveston in 1889), and serves old fashioned ice cream treats such as root beer floats, banana splits, and malts to serve every nostalgic taste.

Local Tip: Head to the back of the store to watch the tasty saltwater taffy being pulled. If you are lucky, the maker might even throw you one!

WATCH THE SUNRISE

Nothing is more amazing then watching the sun rise on a perfect day over the Gulf of Mexico. You have to get up early, but the three cups of coffee it will take to get you moving is a small price to pay for being reminded of how wondrously immense the world is and how small but significant we are in it. Relax and listen to the waves as the red, orange and yellow-hued sun slowly rises, signaling the beginning of a new and glorious day.

Local Tip: Sunrise watching from the Seawall is free! The parking meters are not enforced before 10am.

WAVE FAREWELL TO A
CRUISE SHIP

It may not have been the best show on television, but *The Love Boat* introduced an entire generation to the idea of taking a journey at sea. Whether or not cruising is your thing, it is quite a sight to see these enormous ships slip their lines and head out of the Galveston Channel towards unknown destinations in foreign lands.

Local Tip: Grab a drink in the Olympia Grill, located at Pier 21. This restaurant has outdoor seating and one of the best views of the ships departure.

YAGA'S CHILI QUEST & BEER FEST

Every January the Historic Strand is transformed into a chili cook-off "tasting kitchen" where locals and tourists can sample delicious home-made chili made by contestants from near and far. This recipe for fun also includes refreshing beers, live music, games, and shopping. While the rest of the country digs out from the endless snow, grab your flip flops and heat things up with some of the best chili in Texas.

Local Tip: Pay the extra money and get VIP tickets. You will gain early entry and beat the crowds!

YAGA'S GALVESTON ISLAND WILD TEXAS SHRIMP FESTIVAL

Every September, folks gather on the Historic Strand to celebrate a tiny pink crustacean: the tender and tasty gulf shrimp. This free weekend event features live music, an array of food to accompany the delectable little crustaceans, vendors, a 5K fun run, a kids area, a boat show, and of course - plenty of delicious fresh shrimp.

Local Tip: Buy a gumbo tasting cup ticket in advance, either online or the day of the event. This is the only way to sample the mouthwatering shrimp gumbo along the "gumbo stroll."

Galveston History Scavenger Hunt

- ☐ Oil Rig museum

- ☐ Under the Mardi Gras Arch

- ☐ One of the Historic East End Tree Sculptures

- ☐ Shrimp Boat

- ☐ Garten Verein

- ☐ Ferry Boat

- ☐ Aston Villa

- ☐ Ruins of Pirate Jean LaFitte's house

- ☐ Ike water line on The Historic Strand

- ☐ 1900 storm survivor plaque

- ☐ Bishop's Palace

- ☐ One of the Moody Gardens pyramids

- ☐ Ashbel Smith Building

- ☐ Pleasure Pier

- ☐ Star Drug Store

Galveston Beach Scavenger Hunt

- ☐ Find 3 different types of shells

- ☐ Feed a friendly gull

- ☐ Find a beach umbrella

- ☐ Ask a life guard his or her name

- ☐ Spot a surfer

- ☐ Find a sandcastle higher than 1 foot tall

- ☐ Spot a sailboat

- ☐ Find a live fish

- ☐ Find a live crab

- ☐ Spot a white or brown pelican

- ☐ Find a pair of black flip flops

- ☐ Find a red swim suit

- ☐ Collect something green

- ☐ Spot someone drinking a lemonade

- ☐ Find a bird's foot print in the sand

Galveston Back Streets Scavenger Hunt

☐ Spot a kite

☐ Find a bright yellow house

☐ Find a stop sign

☐ Spot a person riding a bike

☐ Spot a dog

☐ Spot a cat

☐ Find a red car

☐ Find a black truck

☐ Pick a flower

☐ Find a ketchup packet

☐ Pick up a pine cone

☐ Spot a Texas flag

☐ Find 2 different types of leaves

☐ Spot a person wearing a hat

☐ Find a palm tree

Our Favorite Restaurants

Bar 21
2102 Postoffice St
(409)762-2101
Best happy hour

Beerfoot Beach Bar
28th and Seawall Blvd
(409)762-BEER
Best local beers

Board Game Island
213 23rd Street
(409)762-0144
Fun board games

Brew's Brother
2404 Strand
(409)762-BREW
Best bar food

Eatcetera
408 25th Street
(409)762-0803
Best soups

Farley Girls Cafe
801 Postoffice Street
(409)497-4454
Best shrimp and grits

Galvez Bar & Grill
2024 Seawall Blvd
(409)765-7721
Best brunch

Grotto
5222 Seawall Blvd
(800)445-0090
Best Italian cuisine

Gaido's Seafood
3828 Seawall Blvd
(409)762-9625
Best fresh seafood

Jimmy's on the Pier
9001 Seawall Blvd
(409)974-4726
Best over the water

Leon's
55th & Broadway
(409)744-0070
Best BBQ

Little Daddy's Gumbo
2105 Postoffice Street
(409)744-8626
Best gumbo

Maceo Spice & Imports
2706 Market
(409)763-3331
Best muffalettas

Mario's Seawall Italian
628 Seawall Blvd
(409)763-1693
Best pizza

Mosquito Café
628 14th Street
(409)763-1010
Best breakfast

Nonno Tony's
2100 Harborside Dr.
(409)621-5100
Best meatballs

Number 13
7809 Broadway
(409)572-2650
Best steak

Olympia Grill
4908 Seawall Blvd
(409)766-1222
Best greek

PattyCakes Bakery
704 14th Street
(409) 76 Cakes
Best bakery

Queens BBQ
3428 Avenue S
(409)762-3151
Big Texas Style Chili

Rudy & Paco
2028 Postoffice Street
(409)762-3696
Best overall restaurant

Saltwater Grill
2017 Postoffice Street
(409)763-5835
Best fish

Shearn's
7 Hope Blvd
(888)388-8484
Best view

Shrimp 'N Stuff
39th Blvd & Ave O
(409)763-2805
Best local shrimp

ShyKatZ Deli & Bakery
1528 Avenue L & 16th
(409)770-0500
Best sandwich shop

Sky Bar Steak & Sushi
2107 Postoffice Street
(409)621-4Sky
Best sushi

Smooth Tony's
415 9th Street
(409)765-5200
Best patio

Sonny's
1206 19th St
(409)763-9602
Best burger dive

Star Drug Store
510 23rd Street
(409)766-7719
Best milk shakes

The Beach Hut
731 Seawall Blvd
(409)763-6204
Best beach side burger

The Black Pearl Oyster
327 23rd Street
(409)762-7299
Best crab cakes

The Original Mexican
1401 Market Street
(409)762-6001
Best tex mex

The Spot
3204 Seawall Blvd
(409)621-5237
Best family restaurant

The Steakhouse
5222 Seawall Blvd
(800)445-0900
Best wine list

Sunflower Bakery
512 14th Street
(409)763-5500
Best desserts

The Tremont House
2300 Ships Mechanic Row
(409)763-0300
Best rooftop bar

Waterman Restaurant
14302 Steward Road
(409)632-0233
Best by boat

Yaga's Café and Bar
2314 Strand
(409)762-6676
Best local hangout

Hotels

America's Best Value
6302 Seawall Blvd
(409)744-8888

Baymont Inn & Suites
2826 63rd St.
(409)744-3021

Beachcomber Inn
2825 61st St.
(409)744-7133

Candlewood Suites
808 61st St.
(888)230-4134

Casa Del Mar
6102 Seawall Blvd.
(409)740-2431

Comfort Suites
3606 89th Street
(409)741-9977

Commodore
3618 Seawall Blvd.
(409)763-2375

Courtyard Marriott
9550 Seawall Blvd
(409)497-2850

Four Points
2300 Seawall
(409)974-4796

Gaido's Seaside Inn
3700 Seawall Blvd.
(409)762-9625

Galveston Beach Hotel
1702 Seawall Blvd
(409)740-1600

Hampton Inn & Suites
6431 Central City Blvd.
(409)744-0600

Harbor House
2100 Harborside Drive
(409)763-3321

Hilton Galveston Island
5400 Seawall Blvd.
(409)744-5000

Holiday Inn Resort
5002 Seawall Blvd.
(409)740-5300

Holiday Inn Club
11743 San Luis Pass Road
(409)737-2339

Hotel Galvez & Spa:
2024 Seawall Blvd.
(409)765-7721

Inn at the Waterpark
2525 Jones Drive
(409)740-1155

Moody Gardens Hotel,
Seven Hope Blvd.
(409)741-8484

Quality Inn & Suites
5924 Seawall Blvd.
(409)740-1088

Red Roof Inn
5914 Seawall Blvd.
(409)740-1261

Scottish Inns
928 Ferry Road
(409)762-3311

Springhill Suites by Marriott
6303 Broadway
(409)740-9443

Super 8 Motel
2825 1/2 B 61st St.
(409)740-6640

The San Luis Resort
5222 Seawall Blvd
(409)744-1500

The Tremont House:
2300 Mechanic
(409)763-0300

TownePlace Suites
9540 Seawall Blvd
(409)497-2840

The Victorian Resort
6300 Seawall
(409)740-3555

Annual Events

January
Galveston State Park – New Years Run
Houston Happy Hikers run at Mosquito Café
Galveston Restaurant Week
Yaga's Chili Quest & Beer Fest
Special Olympics Texas Polar Plunge at Stewart Beach
Art Walk

February
Mardi Gras
Sea Turtle Saturday

March
Mardi Gras
Home & Garden Show
Causeway FunD Run
Art Walk
Land & Sand 5k&10K

April
The Grand Kids Festival
Lone Star Ironman
FeatherFest & Nature PhotoFest
JA-GA Reggae Festival
Galveston Food & Wine Festival
Adopt A Beach Clean Up
A Bark in the Park
DIVAS Half Marathon &5k

May
Annual Historical Homes Tour
Yaga's Wild Game & BBQ Cook-off
Splash Day
Galveston Island Beach Revue
Sandcastle Competition
Art Walk

June

Sandcastle Competition
Back Garden Tour
Texas Beach Ultimate Fest
Great Texas Catamaran Race
National Juneteenth Celebration
World's Largest Swimming Lesson
Wedding Vow Renewal at Hotel Galvez

July

4th of July Parade and Fireworks
Texas Race Regatta
Art Walk

August

BrewMasters Craft Beer Festival

September

Ironman 5050 Galveston
Galveston Island Wild Texas Shrimp Festival
Adopt a Beach Clean Up
Redfish Rodeo
Gritty Goddess Women's 5K
Ark Walk

October

Life's a Beach Triathlon
Railroad Museum Model Train Show
Halloween Festivities
Bike around the Bay
Harvest Moon Regatta
Toughest 10k Causeway Run
ARToberFEST
WalkAbout
Zombie Zone 5k Survival Challenge
` Feet Beach Cancer
Railroad Museum Hobo Night
Oktoberfest
Ghostly Gardens
Lone Star Motorcycle Rally

November
Veterans Day Salute
Passport to Holiday Magic Events
Moody Gardens Festival of Lights
Home for the Holiday Gift Market
Holiday Half Marathon
Hotel Galvez Holiday Lighting Celebration
Lasers, Lights & Magic in the Park
Art Walk

December
Victorian Homes Tour
Dickens on the Strand
Breakfast with the Sandhill Cranes
Santa Train at Railroad Museum
Santa Hustle Half Marathon & 5k

General Index

**Galveston Island
Historic Tours**
(409)789-9911

**Galveston Island Visitors
Center**
2328 Broadway

**Galveston Railroad
Museum**
2602 Santa Fe Place
(409) 765-5700
galvestonrrmuseum.com

Galveston State Park
14528 Stewart
(409)737-1222
galvestonislandstatepark.org

Garten Verein
2704 Avenue O
(409)765-7834
galvestonhistory.org

Ghost Tours
23rd Street and Sealy Street
(281)658-7254
ghosttourstexas.com

Go Karts
9402 Seawall Blvd
(409)740-6878
galvestongokart.com

**Haunted Mayfield
Manor**
2313 Harborside
(409)762-6677

Hendley Building
20th and Strand

Hotel Galvez
2024 Seawall Blvd
(409) 765-7721
galveston.com/galvez

**Hummel's General Store
& Deli**
13722 Termini San Luis
(409)737-9954

**Karankawa Indian
Campsite and Burial
Ground**
Bob Smith & Jolly Roger
Roads

Katie's Seafood
1902 Wharf Rd
(409)763-8160
katiesseafoodmarket.com

Kites Unlimited
8910 Seawall Blvd
(409)744-4121

La Kings Confectionery
2323 Strand Street
(409) 762-6100
lakingsconfectionery.com

Magic Carpet Mini Golf
9030 Seawall Blvd
(409)740-2000

Moody Gardens
One Hope Blvd
1-800-582-4673
moodygardens.com

Moody Gardens Golf Course
1700 Sydnor
(409)683-GOLF
moodygardensgolf.com

Moody Mansion
2618 Broadway
(409)762-7668
www.moodymansion.org

Murdoch's
2215 Seawall Blvd
(409)762-7478

Nautical Antiques
2202 Mechanic
(409)539-5469

Ocean Star Offshore Drilling Rig & Museum,
Pier 19
(409)766-7827
oceanstaroec.com

Old City Cemetery
On Broadway
Between 40th and 43rd St

Old Red
914--916 Ave. B

Ohana Surf & Skate
2814 Ave R ½
(409)763-2700
www.ohanasurfandskate.com

Pier 21 Theater
2100 Harborside Drive
Galveston, Texas
(409)763-3808

Ruins of Pirate Jean Lafitte's House
1417 Harborside Drive

Rosenberg Library
2310 Sealy St
(409) 763-8854
rosenberg-library.org

Sacred Heart Church
1302 Broadway St.
(409)762-9646
holyfamilygb.org

Schlitterbahn
2026 Lockheed St
(409)762-9283
schlitterbahn.com

Sea n Sand
4127 Pirates Beach
(409)771-2649
www.seansand.com

Seawolf Park
(409)797-5114
cavalla.org

About the Authors

Darcie and her mom, Natalie, emigrated to Texas from the far North Left Coast of the U.S. over the course of many years, finally landing in the Houston area starting some 20 years ago. They turned their love of travel into a web site focused on trips for women (Great Girl Trips) and their love of the water, sand and sun into places in Galveston's Pirate's Beach, Jamaica Beach and Tiki Island. This book was written in response to countless discussions with friends about Galveston's many charms beyond the beach ("Sure, but did you know...?"). If you see them out and about while exploring the island (and you will!), make sure to buy them a glass of wine and ask them about the many other great places tucked away in Galveston's secret and not so secret corners.

CPSIA information can be obtained at www.ICGtesting.com
Printed in the USA
LVOW02s1504210415

435483LV00012B/58/P